Animal Homes

# Ants and Their Nests

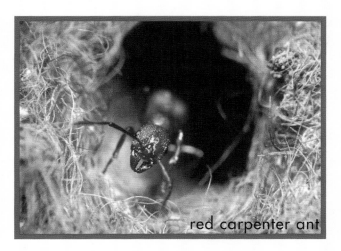

red carpenter ant

by Linda Tagliaferro

Consulting Editor: Gail Saunders-Smith, Ph.D.

Consultant: Gary A. Dunn, Director of Education
Young Entomologists' Society
Lansing, Michigan

Capstone
press

Mankato, Minnesota

Pebble Plus is published by Capstone Press,
151 Good Counsel Drive, P.O. Box 669, Mankato, Minnesota 56002.

9  V008  15  14  13

*Library of Congress Cataloging-in-Publication Data*
Tagliaferro, Linda.
    Ants and their nests / by Linda Tagliaferro.
    p. cm.—(Pebble Plus, Animal homes)
    Summary: Simple text and photographs describe ants and the nests in which they live.
    Includes bibliographical references (p. 23) and index.
    ISBN 0-7368-2380-8 (hardcover)
    ISBN 0-7368-5120-8 (paperback)
    1. Ants—Nests—Juvenile literature. [1. Ants—Nests. 2. Ants—Habits and behavior.]
I. Title. II. Series.
QL568.F7T24 2004
595.79'6—dc22                                                    2003013421

**Editorial Credits**

Martha E. H. Rustad, editor; Linda Clavel, series designer; Deirdre Barton and Wanda Winch,
        photo researchers; Karen Risch, product planning editor

**Photographs**

Every effort has been made to secure permission and provide appropriate credit for photographic material. The
publisher deeply regrets any omission and pledges to correct errors called to its attention in subsequent editions.

Unless otherwise acknowledged, all photographs are the property of Scott Foresman, a division of Pearson
Education.

Photo locators denoted as follow: Top (T), Center (C), Bottom (B), Left (L), Right (R), Background (Bkgd).

Cover: ©George B. Diebold/Corbis; 1 ©Joe McDonald; 5 ©John Mitchell/Bruce Colman Inc.; 7 ©Frans
Lanting/Minden Pictures; 9 ©Gerry Ellis/Minden Pictures; 11©Konrad Wothe/Minden Pictures; 13 ©Milton
Rand; 15 ©Mark Moffett/Minden Pictures; 17©Anthony Bannister/Gallo Images/Corbis; 19©Biophoto/Van
Baelinghem Thierry/Peter Arnold, Inc.; 21 ©Michael Rose/Frank Lane Pictures Agency/Corbis

# Table of Contents

# Building Nests

Ants live in nests. Ants build their nests in the spring or fall.

Some ants build nests
in five days. Other ants
take months to build
their nests.

Some ants build nests
with leaves and sticky silk.
Other ants build nests
in soil or wood.

tailor ants ➤

Ants dig tunnels underground or inside trees. They build chambers in the tunnels. Ants store food and raise their young in the chambers.

yellow ants ➤

# Colonies and Eggs

A colony is a group of ants
living together in a nest.
Hundreds and thousands
of ants live in a colony.

red ants ▶

13

The queen ant lays her eggs in the nest. Worker ants take care of young ants.

fire ants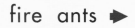

14

# Staying Safe

Some ants close the opening
to their nest with pebbles.
The pebbles keep out
other animals.

harvester ants ▶

Some ants put twigs on top
of their nests. The twigs
keep out rain.

# A Good Home

Different kinds of ants build different kinds of nests. Nests are good homes for ants.

fire ant nest ▶

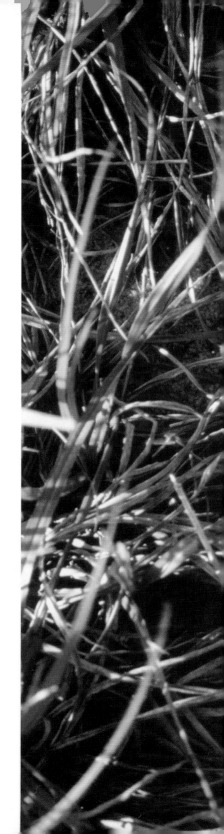

# Glossary

**chamber**—a room in an ant nest

**colony**—a large group of animals that live together; thousands of ants live together in some colonies.

**queen ant**—an adult female ant that lays eggs; most colonies have only one queen ant.

**silk**—a sticky fiber made by some ants

**tunnel**—a passage under the ground

**twig**—a small stick or branch

**worker ant**—an adult female ant that does not lay eggs; worker ants build nests and take care of young ants.

# Read More

**Frost, Helen.** *Leaf-Cutting Ants.* Rain Forest Animals. Mankato, Minn.: Pebble Books, 2003.

**Loewen, Nancy.** *Tiny Workers: Ants in Your Backyard.* Backyard Bugs. Minnneapolis: Picture Window Books, 2003.

**Robinson, W. Wright.** *How Insects Build Their Amazing Homes.* Animal Architects. Woodbridge, Conn.: Blackbirch Press, 1999.

# Index/Word List